Kentucky State Parks

Kris; David

Merry Christmas! 1991

Judy; Tom

KENTUCKY

STATE PARKS

RECREATION

HERITAGE

BEAUTY

WILDERNESS

KENTUCKY STATE PARKS

Judy King Cowgill

Produced in association with

Harmony House
Publishers – Louisville

This book is dedicated to my parents, Hilda and Sam King, who instilled in me a love of Kentucky, and to my husband, Norwood, and daughters Kimberly, Cynthia, and Christine, who shared with me many wonderful experiences at the Kentucky State Parks.

I would like to thank Kentucky's Department of Tourism and Department of Parks for their cooperation in the production of this book. In particular, I owe my gratitude to the hard-working, dedicated, enthusiastic park superintendents, with whom I visited at each of the parks. Their knowledge was fundamental to the success of this book.

Executive Editors: William Butler and William Strode
Library of Congress Catalog Number: 91-75133
Hardcover International Standard Book Number 1-56469-000-8
Printed in U.S.A.
First Edition printed Fall, 1991 by Judy King Cowgill and Harmony House Publishers,
P.O. Box 90, Prospect, Kentucky 40059 (502) 228-2010 / 228-4446
Copyright © 1991 by Judy King Cowgill
Photographs copyright © 1991 by the individual photographers.

CONTENTS

INTRODUCTION

The Kentucky State Parks are known as the "nation's finest." After spending two years in research for this book, and traveling 6703 miles visiting each and every park, I heartily agree.

Kentucky is steeped in history and unsurpassed in beauty. Combined with the many breathtaking lakes in the state, these factors make for the settings of all the state parks.

The Kentucky State Park system became a reality in 1924, due largely to the efforts of one man, Dr. Willard Rouse Jillson. Dr. Jillson was the State Geologist in Kentucky and was recognized throughout the country as outstanding in his field. He was appointed the first Park Director and was Chairman of the first State Park Commission. Since little money was available in those early days, Dr. Jillson began speaking around the state, getting communities involved in obtaining land for use as State Parks.

The criteria he developed for choosing a state park site were its natural beauty, its state and/or national history, a well balanced selection of land over the entire state, and the cooperation of local citizens to deed land for public use. Kentucky needed jobs and revenue, and not only did the state parks provide both, they also helped each state park area generate other means of commerce. Restaurants, gift shops, gasoline stations, and lodging outside the parks were all begun by private investors to meet the needs of visitors.

Today the Kentucky State Park system boasts forty-four parks, plus the Kentucky Horse Park.

The park system is divided into three categories. The premier parks are called Kentucky Resort Parks. These parks contain everything a visitor needs for an extended vacation. There is overnight lodging in the form of rooms and cottages, campgrounds, dining, and a wide variety of recreational activities. Most contain a golf course and are situated on a lake for boating, fishing, and swimming. Their natural settings in the mountains or on one of Kentucky's beautiful lakes provide beautiful, restful surroundings.

The second group of parks are called Recreational Parks. These are similar in nature to the Resort Parks, except that they provide only campgrounds, with no overnight lodging or dining facilities. Most of these parks are situated on a lake for convenient water activities.

The third group of parks are called State Historic Sites. These parks are small in acreage, but hold some historical signifcance. There is always something to learn at the Historic Parks.

Whatever your pleasure, Kentucky State Parks can fulfill your need for relaxation, recreation, enjoyment, beauty, and history. I hope you will take time to visit all the parks, either as a citizen of Kentucky or as a visitor. Southern hospitality is at its best at the Kentucky State Parks, the "nation's finest."

Located in the Daniel Boone National Forest, Cumberland Falls State Resort Park is twenty miles southwest of Corbin, Kentucky on Kentucky 90. Access is off I-75 and U.S. 25 W. Called the "Niagara of the South" the falls takes its name from the Cumberland River. The falls are normally 68 feet high and 125 feet wide in summer, but at flood stage may be 300 feet wide.

The beautiful Cumberland Falls boasts the only "moonbow" in the western hemisphere. The only other one in the world is Victoria Falls in Zimbabwe, Africa. The arch of white light from the base of the falls to downstream can be seen when there is a full moon on a clear evening. This unusual feature, along with the wild life, and geological features of sandstone, make a wonderful setting for the park.

Shawnee Indians first roamed this area and considered the falls a sacred place. Dr. Thomas Walker, the first settler in Kentucky, came in 1750 and named the river after the Duke of Cumberland.

The first permanent landowners in the area were Mary and Lewis Renfro, who in 1850 built a small log cabin beside the falls. Over the next 25 years, they enlarged their home, and provided lodging for those who wished to fish.

Renfro eventually sold his land to one Socrates Owens, who built the Cumberland Falls Hotel on the Renfro log cabin site.

In 1902, a Mr. Brunson bought the hotel, changed the name, and ran the Brunson Hotel, later called Moonbow Inn, for thirty years.

In the early 1930s there was controversy between preservationists and the Cumberland River Power Company which wanted to build a hydroelectric dam above the falls. Afraid of losing the beauty of the area, Senator DuPont of Delaware, who had visited the falls often, offered to buy the falls and surrounding property and donate them to the state.

On January 29, 1931, the CRPC conveyed the holdings to Kentucky. DuPont's heirs (he had died while settling the issue) purchased 593 acres for $400,000. Cumberland Falls State Resort Park was dedicated August 21, 1931, the third state park in the system.

The Civilian Conservation Corps (C.C.C.) had two camps of 200 men in the area during the Depression. A better road was built, fifteen cabins were made, and DuPont Lodge, a rustic log structure with 26 rooms, was constructed one half mile from the falls. Six years later it burned. The WPA rebuilt the lodge, this time using more sandstone, and the new building was dedicated in 1942.

Today the park boasts 1657 acres. Facilities and recreation are abundant. The lodge now has 52 rooms with a 300 seat dining area and meeting rooms. There are also 20 woodland rooms, 11 efficiency cottages, 7 one-bedroom and 9 two-bedroom cottages. Overnight one may also stay in the fifty-site campground with water and electrical hookups.

For convenience there is a grocery store in the campground, and a coffee shop and a log cabin gift shop by the falls. The Bob Blair Museum has Indian artifacts, information on plants and animals, and a history of the park.

Recreation, most of it seasonal, includes horseback riding, swimming in an olympic size pool, game room, tennis, fishing, rafting, horseshoes, picnicking with shelters, playgrounds, and shuffleboard. There are seventeen miles of hiking trails with various degrees of difficulty. A full time naturalist and recreational director are at the park to assist.

Special Events include a Kentucky Hills Craft Weekend in March, a Photography Weekend in April, a River Cleanup Project in May, a C.C.C. Reunion in October, a New Year's Eve Party and a Valentine Party.

CUMBERLAND FALLS

Virginia Sellards Wiley, known as Jenny Wiley, was a legendary pioneer woman who lived in the area of Kentucky now known as Jenny Wiley State Resort Park.

Hers is a story of hardship and loss, the death of family members to marauding Indians, captivity at the hands of an Indian chief for 11 months, escape from her captor and eventual reuniting with her family and triumph in the unforgiving wilderness.

Her legend inspired the name of this park, which is located in eastern Kentucky three miles west of Prestonsburg off U.S. 23/460 on Kentucky 3. The park, opened in 1962, features a convention center and lots of recreation. There is a game room, gift shop, miniature golf, a grocery, nine hole golf course with pro shop and rental carts and clubs, picnic grounds, shelters, playgrounds, community pool, shuffleboard, and many miles of hiking trails. A recreational director oversees these activities. In addition, there is a sky lift that goes to the top of Sugar Camp Mountain, where views can be seen as far away as sixty miles.

The park features a two hundred mile trail named in Jenny Wiley's honor. The hiking trail starts at the park and ends at South Portsmouth, Kentucky. Several hundred adventurous people trek it each year.

For evening entertainment there is the 800-seat outdoor amphitheater. The Jenny Wiley Theatre Company rotates Broadway plays and The Story of Jenny from June through August, Tuesday through Sunday. Other Special Events are Old Christmas in January, and the Kentucky Highlands Folk Festival with arts and crafts, music and storytelling in September.

The park is located on the edge of the 1150 acre Dewey Lake, named in honor of Admiral George Dewey. The lake has forty miles of shoreline and is fifty feet deep at the base of the dam. There is a full marina with 199 slips and rental pontoons, pedal boats, and fishing boats. Fishing is good for largemouth, smallmouth and rock bass, bluegill, catfish, crappie and muskie.

Jenny Wiley State Resort Park is open year round. The May Lodge, named for a local Congressman, has 49 rooms with a pool, a dining room seating 224 and meeting rooms. There are seventeen one and two-bedroom cottages and a 126 site campground with utilities, opened on a seaonal basis.

JENNY WILEY

The names of Greenup County and Boyd County were combined to produce the word "Greenbo", used in naming Greenbo Lake State Resort Park. Located in northeastern Kentucky on Kentucky 1, eight miles southeast of Greenup via I-64, the park has the fourth largest acreage in the system at 3008. There is an abundance of animal life and wildflowers in the predominately forested park.

Originally started by the Greenbo Recreation Association as a local park, the state was given the land in 1955 and opened the park in 1960. A 225-acre lake, fed by three streams, opened in 1958. Greenbo Lake was made for fishing; a record largemouth bass of thirteen pounds and eight ounces was caught in these waters.

On the grounds of the park are the restored remnants of a one-room schoolhouse and the Buffalo Furnace, built by a community of settlers in the early 1800s.

Also on the grounds of the park is the beautiful, rustic Jesse Stuart Lodge. Stuart, a famous Kentucky poet and author, was born in Greenup County, where he lived his entire life. His home is just outside the park. The Lodge opened in 1971 and has 36 rooms with private balconies or patios overlooking the lake. Inside is the 232-seat dining room open year round, meeting rooms and a gift shop. One may also stay in the 63-site campground which has water and electrical hookups and two service buildings, open from April 1 to October 31.

Recreation includes basketball, bike rentals, a game room, miniature golf, picnic areas and shelters, playgrounds, shuffleboard, tennis, swimming and horseback riding, with a full time recreational director. The lake offers fishing for black bass, bluegill, catfish and rainbow trout. A 65-slip marina provides pontoons, pedal boats, rowboats, canoes and motorboats.

The Michael Tygart Trail System, named for an early Kentucky settler, links with the longer Jenny Wiley Trail in the park. There are several hikes available, the longest being 24 miles.

Special Events include a story-telling week and a Railroad Appreciation week in March. In September there is a weekend dedicated to an appreciation of Jesse Stuart, his life and books. Fall brings an arts and crafts festival in October and a 5-K run in December.

GREENBO LAKE

Lake Barkley was built by the United States Army Corps of Engineers, and completed in July, 1966. The earth and concrete dam was built for flood control, recreation, and for freedom of navigation along the river. The lake was named for former Kentucky Senator and Vice President of the United States, Alben Barkley. Lake Barkley comprises 57,920 acres with a shoreline 1004 miles long and connects to Kentucky Lake by a canal, making the two lakes together the largest man-made body of water in the world. The lake is known for its good fishing, duck hunting, and bird-watching for golden and bald eagles.

Lying in the gently rolling hills of southwest Kentucky on the eastern shore of Lake Barkley, Lake Barkley State Resort Park was opened year round on December 1, 1967. The state leases 1800 acres from the Corps and owns the rest of the land, for a total of 3600 acres in the park. The park provides a full service marina with 60 open slips and 112 covered slips, pontoon boats, ski boats, and jet skis. Fishing is for bass, crappie, catfish, rockfish, and sauger. There is also a sand beach.

Other recreational facilities at Lake Barkley State Resort Park include an 18-hole golf course with pro shop and rental clubs and carts, nine miles of hiking trails, horseback riding, picnic areas and shelters, playgrounds, four tennis courts, basket-ball courts, shuffleboard, the only trapshooting range in the park system, and an indoor fitness center with nautilus equipment, racquetball, aerobics instruction, tanning beds, sauna, steam room, and whirlpool.

Overnight accomodations at Lake Barkley State Resort Park include the four star Barkley Lodge. Dedicated on June 1, 1970, this unique building was designed by New York architect Edward Durrell Stone. It is made of western cedar, Douglas fir, and three and a half acres of glass. The 120-room, four suite lodge is built in a half circle around the lake shoreline and all rooms have a view of Lake Barkley. The lodge has a dining room seating 331, coffee shop, game room, gift shop, pool and meeting rooms.

Other accomodations include Little River Lodge (10 rooms and one suite), named for the river that runs into the Cumberland, thirteen two-bedroom cottages, and an eighty-site campground with water and electricity. There is a full time recreational director, a convention center seating one thousand, and a 4800 foot lighted airstrip.

Lake Barkley State Resort Park is located 29 miles west of Hopkinsville on Kentucky 1489 off 68W. Special Events include Barkley Bash on New Years Eve, Sweetheart Weekend, Eagle Weekend and two golf events.

LAKE BARKLEY

Barkley Lodge

More than twenty caverns surround the area in northeastern Kentucky known as Carter Caves State Park. Located off I-64, 38 miles west of Ashland on Kentucky 182 north, the 1350 acre park has unusual rock outcroppings, natural bridges, caves and lots of rare plants and animals.

Local residents originally used the land for an area park, and in 1946 the state bought the property and officially opened the state park in 1952.

In 1962, Caveland Lodge, a 28-room fieldstone building was constructed, along with fifteen cottages. Housed in the lodge is an 198-seat dining room, a gift shop and two meeting rooms, as well as a comfortable lobby. There is a pool for guests. Available also is a 95-site camping area with water and electrical hookups, open from April 1 to October 31.

The park has many recreational activities. There is a nine hole golf course with rentals available, more than six miles of nature trails, picnic areas with shelters, a playground, miniature golf, a community pool, two tennis courts and horseback riding.

In addition to the above, there is the 45-acre Smokey Lake, an impoundment of Tygert Creek, with boating and fishing for bass, brim, catfish, crappie, and muskie.

Carter Caves State Park also contains several natural bridges. Located in Tygert State Forest, there is Smokey Bridge, the largest natural bridge in Kentucky, and Carter Caves Natural Bridge, the only one in Kentucky with a paved road on top.

But by far the biggest attraction in the area is the caves. Casual and serious spelunkers come from all over to tour the caverns. There is a Welcome Center, built years ago, with a gift shop, information, and tickets to four caves. There are special tours arranged for anyone with experience, given by a full time naturalist or recreation director. A back-packing permit is required.

Saltpetre Cave involves early Kentucky history. Near the entrance, there is a name and date written on the wall — "Simon Kenton, 1783," an early Kentucky pioneer. During the War of 1812, gunpowder was made in the cave.

X-Cave was discovered in the 1860s, and so named for its X-shaped formations and shapes of passages. There are luminous fans, pipes and spirals in stone formed millions of years ago. There are some bats and an underground lake.

Bat Cave is the largest cave in the park. Open only in the summer, it is the winter home to 40,000 Indiana bats. There are two and a half miles of charted passages.

Cascade Cave is exceptionally beautiful and by far the most popular of the caves. Features include a thirty-foot high underground waterfall and lots of formations. The three-fourths mile passage stays 50 to 60 degrees year round.

Three Special Events occur at Carter Caves State Park: The Crawl-a-Thon, held in February, is a three-day event for spelunkers; the International Strange Music Weekend: and the Mountain Memories Weekend, devoted to mountain music.

The park is open every day except for Christmas.

CARTER CAVES

The Mountain Laurel Festival

Pine Mountain State Resort Park claims the honor for being the first Kentucky state park.

In 1924, Dr. Willard Rouse Jillson, a renowned geologist, was in the area looking for land for a park. The citizens of Bell County donated the acres on Pine Mountain, overlooking the valley of the Kentucky Ridge State Forest, to the state. When Dr. Jillson headed the first State Park Commission in 1925, "Cumberland State Park," as Pine Mountain was first called, became the first in a long line of parks. It officially opened in 1926, and changed its name in 1938.

Pine Mountain State Resort Park is located fifteen miles north of Middlesboro off U.S. 25E in Pineville at the top of Pine Mountain. This range of mountains is over 125 miles long. Almost fifty percent of the forest is Eastern Hemlock pine trees. There is still virgin timber here, some estimated to be 250-350 years old.

In 1938 the first office/lodge was erected, as well as several one-bedroom log cottages. The present lodge was built in 1963 and was named for Herndon J. Evans, an early supporter of the park. Today there are thirty rooms with private balconies, ten one-bedroom and ten two-bedroom cottages, open all year. A campground with modest facilities is available from April 1 to October 31. There is also a dining room seating 216, a gift shop, and a meeting room for 150.

The 1519 acre park has lots of recreational activities, supervised by a full time naturalist and a part-time recreational director. The nine hole golf course has rental carts and clubs. There is also miniature golf, picnic areas with shelters, playgrounds, shuffleboard, a pool , volleyball and basketball courts, a game room, and a small amphitheater.

There are nine miles of hiking trails in the forests, especially beautiful in the fall. Sights to see are wildlife such as deer, bobcat, fox and turkey, rock shelter houses, two natural bridges, Indian artifacts, abundant wild flowers, a chained rock (above the city of Pineville which citizens "chained" in 1933), a fern garden, a hemlock garden, honeymoon falls, and a nature preserve to protect the timber. There is also a nature center with local history, plants and animals.

The 3000 seat Laurel Cove Amphitheater is the setting for the famous Mountain Laurel Festival held in late May. Originally begun to honor Dr. Thomas Walker, the first settler in Kentucky, it is now also held to enjoy the beauty of the Mountain Laurel. The week-long event, begun in 1935, features arts and crafts, a 5-K race, and a Grand Ball. A queen is crowned from representatives of all the colleges and universities across the state. Other Special Events include a Photography Weekend in May, a Bluegrass Festival in August, and the Great Dulcimer Convention in September.

PINE MOUNTAIN

Chained Rock

Pennyroyal, sometimes called Pennyrile, is an annual pale violet flower. It is found from July through September in the region of the 15,331 acre Pennyrile Forest, from which Pennyrile Forest State Resort Park takes its name. The park is located off the Western Kentucky Turnpike on Kentucky 109 between the cities of Dawson Springs and Hopkinsville.

The park opened in 1937. A rustic wood and stone lobby and cabins were built first. In 1962, the 24-room lodge was built overlooking the lake.

The park now boasts 863 acres with a tranquil setting and recreation for all. The lake provides rental boats and paddleboats. There is fishing for largemouth bass, bluegill, catfish and crappie. A beach for swimming is on the lake. Other activities include a 9-hole golf course with pro shop and rental clubs and carts, miniature golf, picnic grounds, shelters, a playground, a pool, two tennis courts, shuffleboard, and a game room.

There are seven miles of hiking trails through the Pennyrile Forest, the longest being one and one-half miles. A naturalist is available year round as well as a part-time recreational director.

The park is open from March 1 to December 19.

PENNYRILE

Nestled in the eastern Kentucky foothills of the Cumberland Plateau at the northern portion of the Daniel Boone National Forest is Buckhorn Lake State Resort Park. It is located 25 miles northwest of Hazard, Kentucky.

The unusual name derives from the discovery of a buck's horn by a nearby salt lick; hence the name of the town, the lake and finally, the park

The United States Army Corps of Engineers built the 1200 acre Buckhorn lake, after constructing a rock-fill dam on the middle fork of the Kentucky River. The state leased the land from the Corps and in 1964 opened Buckhorn Lake State Park with 856 acres. A lodge was built and dedicated in that year.

The park has a full-time recreational director. The lake provides fishing for large and smallmouth bass, bluegill, catfish, crappie and muskie, with fishing boats and pontoons available for rental. Other recreation includes a beach, bike rentals, a game room, over two miles of hiking trails, miniature golf, picnicking, a playground, a pool, shuffleboard, basketball courts, and two tennis courts.

There are special events occuring every month the park is open from March until Christmas.

BUCKHORN LAKE

Lake Cumberland provides a beautiful setting for Lake Cumberland State Resort Park. It is located south of the Cumberland Parkway, 14 miles southeast of Jamestown off U.S. Highway 127 in south central Kentucky, 20 miles north of the Tennessee border.

Dr. Thomas Walker first saw the Cumberland River in 1750. On a bluff overlooking the river, he named it after the Duke of Cumberland, son of George II of England. Two hundred years later, Wolf Creek Dam was constructed by the United States Army Corps of Engineers, creating Cumberland Lake. Now the lake is 101 miles long with over 50,000 acres of water and 1255 miles of shoreline. The average depth is 90 feet, the deepest point being 185 feet. There are cliffs, wildlife, and sheltered caves all along the lake, as well as government and privately-owned facilities. It is without doubt one of the finest fishing and recreational lakes in all of the eastern United States.

The 3000-acre park is on a narrow strip of land with water on three sides. This accounts for its abundance of wildlife. The animals are protected, and there is plenty of food to sustain deer, raccoons, gray fox, and more.

On January 1, 1951, the Secretary of the Army granted 2791 acres of land for the park to the Commonwealth of Kentucky, and a small lodge was begun and completed in 1953. This first building was called Lure Lodge, after the fine fishing on Lake Cumberland, but was later renamed Pumpkin Creek Lodge and renovated in 1989 with 13 rooms.

A new Lure Lodge was completed September 8, 1962, and there are still additions being made. There are now 63 rooms overlooking the lake, with a gift shop, game room, meeting rooms, lounge area and a 234-seat dining room.

In addition to the two lodges, there are 30 one and two-bedroom cottages, and a camping area with water and electricity, open from April 1 to November 30.

Recreational facilities abound for the over one million visitors each year. There are 150 slips for all types of rental boats. Houseboats, ski boats, pontoons, canoes, and fishing boats are all available for hourly, daily, or weekly rental. Fishing is great for bass, bluegill, crappie, rainbow trout, rockfish, and walleye. Other facilities include a nine-hole par three golf course, lighted miniature golf, nature trails including a four mile loop trail through beech, oak and hickory forests, picnicking, playgrounds, shuffleboard, horseback riding, tennis, a nature center, and planned recreation. In addition to the community pool, there is an indoor pool facility — the only one in the state park system. The building is temperature-controlled, with skylights, an atrium, a lounge, a spa, and an exercise room.

The park is open all year. Special Events include a Senior Citizens Package in October and a Fall Fishing Derby.

LAKE CUMBERLAND

The Old Time Fiddlers Contest

The U.S. Army Corps of Engineers created the recreational and flood control lake, Rough River, with a dam on the river of the same name.

In 1962 the Kentucky Department of Parks leased 637 acres on the 5000 acre lake and built Rough River Dam State Resort Park. Its overnight facilities include a 40-room lodge, 15 two-bedroom cottages and 66 campsites with water and electricity, open from April 1 to October 31.

Open all year, the park has a marina with 165 open slips, 30 open houseboat slips, and 48 covered slips. Available to rent are fishing boats, pontoons, rowboats and pedal boats. There is fishing for bass, bluegill, catfish, crappie, rough fish and walleye. A cruise boat, "Lady of the Lake", takes daily excursions on the water. A beach with a concession stand is open to the public in the summer.

A full-time recreational director provides help with other activities, such as miniature golf, shuffleboard, ping pong, horseshoes, volleyball and basketball. A nine-hole par three golf course has a pro shop with rental clubs and carts. There is a one mile hiking trail and a fitness trail with exercise stations. There are picnic areas with shelters and playgrounds. The lodge has a pool, a gift shop, meeting rooms, and a dining room seating 209.

The park is in western Kentucky on Kentucky 79 via the Western Kentucky Turnpike. A lighted airstrip, 2500 feet in length, is on park grounds.

Special Events include a Sport Aviation Week in September with home-built planes, remote control planes, and other aerial displays. In July the park hosts the Official Kentucky State Championship Old Time Fiddlers Contest.

ROUGH RIVER

Kenlake State Resort Park is located on the middle western shore of Kentucky Lake, where Kentucky Dam was originally to be built. It is forty miles southwest of Paducah, off I-24, the Purchase Parkway, and U.S. 68E. The state leased the 1795 acres and dedicated a park there in 1948.

The only state park to have a lodging facility with a hotel (interior doors) design, Kenlake Hotel was completed in 1952. It has dining for 225, a pool, a game room, a gift shop and meeting rooms. In addition to the 48-room hotel, there are 34 one, two, and three bedroom cottages. A full-service campground with 92 sites is open from April 1 to October 31.

Because of its location on Kentucky Lake, there is a full service marina with 76 open slips and 130 covered slips. There is fishing for bass, bluegill, catfish, crappie, rockfish, and sauger. Rental boats available include houseboats, fishing boats, pontoons, and ski boats. Because of the size of Kentucky Lake, this is the best spot in the state for big boat sailing. Regattas are popular in the summer. A beach is on the park grounds for swimming.

Kenlake State Resort Park has four indoor tennis courts with pro shop and rental rackets. It is the only indoor facility for tennis in the state park system. Five outdoor courts are at the park also. Other activities include a nine hole golf course with pro shop and rental carts and clubs, a hiking trail, picnic grounds with shelters and playgrounds, and shuffleboard. There is a grocery in the park.

Open year round, Kenlake State Resort Park offers a Blues Music Festival in August. The park is also only minutes away from Land Between the Lakes, a 170,000-acre national recreation area.

KENLAKE

One of the Tennessee Valley Authority's mandates upon establishment in 1933 was the management of the Tennessee River flood plain. To that end, the TVA constructed a massive dam on the river over a six-year period, creating Kentucky Lake. The dam, dedicated by President Harry Truman in 1945, is the largest dam built by TVA, stretching a mile and one-half long and 206 feet high.

Kentucky Lake is the largest man-made lake in the eastern part of the United States, encompassing 160,000 acres of water. With a canal connecting neighboring Lake Barkley, the two lakes comprise one of the largest man-made waterway area in the world.

The TVA built a small village to house the workers during the construction years. Upon completion of the project, the village was sold to the state. Kentucky then upgraded the existing buildings and area, and opened Kentucky Dam Village State Resort Park on May 19, 1948. The park, open year round, is located 21 miles southeast of Paducah off I-24. It is the only park to start with a major group of existing buildings and is the most developed park in the system with 1351 acres.

Kentucky Dam Village State Resort Park now boasts more lodging space than any other state park. The Village Inn Lodge opened in July 1962 and has 72 rooms overlooking Kentucky Lake. There is a dining room, a gift shop, meeting rooms and a pool. The Village Green Inn, once the hospital for the TVA, has 14 rooms. There are 67 one, two, and three bedroom cottages. Many are renovated from the original village. Twenty are executive cottages built for the Southern Governor's Conference in 1967. The camping area is on the former grounds of the town of Gilbertsville, which was razed to create the lake and campground. It has 221 campsites with water and electricity.

Kentucky Dam Village State Resort Park has a full service marina, the largest in the state park system, with 93 open slips and 138 covered slips. Rental boats consist of fishing boats, pontoons, rowboats, ski boats, houseboats and paddle boats. Fishing is good for bass, bluegill, catfish, crappie and rockfish. A beach is on the lake.

An 18-hole golf course, with pro shop and rental clubs and carts is rated by the P.G.A. as one of the top 200 golf courses in the nation. There is also a convention center seating 900, a row of shops, a game room with full-time recreational director, miniature golf, tennis courts, courts for basketball, volleyball, and badminton, shuffleboard, riding stables, picnic areas, shelters, and playgrounds, and an airstrip with a 4000 foot lighted runway.

Special Events include the Buffalo Weekend in February, the Joe Creason Golf Tournament in May, a Septemberfest, and a Valentine Weekend.

KENTUCKY DAM VILLAGE

A fishing tournament on the lake

One of the wonders of the world surely must be Natural Bridge. This sandstone arch is said to be a million years old, spanning 78 feet in length, 65 feet in height, 12 feet thick and 20 feet wide. It was created over a period of sixty million years of erosion by the Red River and its tributaries. While Natural Bridge is neither the largest, the oldest, nor the most accessible of the 150 natural stone arches in the area, it is by far the most famous, having been a tourist attraction since 1889.

In that year the Kentucky Union Railway Company built a line through Slade, Kentucky for timbermen who were coming to speculate on logging contracts. The Railway Company saw a potential for tourism in the area and built a park with picnic areas, a campground, and a trail to Natural Bridge. In 1923 the first Hemlock Lodge was built. Made of logs, it remained until 1968 when it burned. The park itself, later owned by the Louisville and Nashville Railroad, was donated to the state in 1926, just after the park system became a reality, making it one of the four original state parks.

Natural Bridge State Resort Park is located off the Mountain Parkway on Kentucky 11 just south of Slade in the heart of the Daniel Boone National Forest in east central Kentucky. The 1647 acre park, open year round, is unique for its hiking trails, with over eighteen miles of walking to Natural Bridge, Lovers Leap, Devils Gulch and Lookout Point. Other activities include miniature golf, tennis, swimming, and traveling by sky lift, ascending within six hundred feet of Natural Bridge. There is a four-acre pond with pedal boats and Millcreek Lake, a 54-acre water area for canoes, rowboats and fishing for bream, catfish, crappie, bass, and rainbow trout. The one-acre Hoedown Island in the middle of the pond is the scene of square dancing in the evening. An activities building houses a nature museum and auditorium.

The new Hemlock Lodge, built in 1962, is on a ledge overlooking a deep valley. It is circled by native hemlocks. The lodge has 35 rooms, a 155-seat dining room, a gift shop and meeting rooms. There are six efficiencies and four one-bedroom cottages. Two campgrounds with 95 sites, water and electrical hookups, and two service buildings are open seasonally, with a full-time recreational director.

The middle fork of the Red River runs through the park. The Kentucky Nature Preserves Commission has set aside 994 acres of the park for a state nature preserve. As is expected, Special Events are geared toward nature. Subjects include a wildflower weekend, a mushroom weekend, and a photography weekend.

NATURAL BRIDGE

The Red River Gorge

The Red River

The area known in Kentucky as "The Barrens" is the setting for Barren River State Resort Park. The name derives from early settlers' initial descriptions of the land, misunderstanding that native Indians burned large expanses of the forest to provide grazing areas for buffalo herds. The name stuck despite the area's obvious green and lush condition.

The park is located in south central Kentucky, 95 miles south of Louisville. Access to the park is from I-65, onto the Cumberland Parkway to US highway 31E.

In 1960, construction began on a 146 foot-high dam on the Barren River. The Louisville District of the United States Army Corps of Engineers designed, built and now operate Barren River Lake. In October, 1964 the 10,000 acre lake was operational, with 141 miles of shoreline and an average depth of 35 feet.

The people of Barren County wanted to locate a state park by their new lake, and the state obliged by buying several farms adjacent to the lake. The Corps of Engineers donated additional land, and the Barren River State Resort Park was established on January 1, 1965.

This park resort is the most recent to be established. The boat dock opened in 1966 with a marina. Fishing boats, pontoons and houseboats may be rented. Individuals fish for bass, bluegill, catfish, crappie, muskie, rough fish and walleye. There are picnic shelters and a 99-site campground with electricity and water hookups.

Over the years, numerous recreational facilities have been added. In addition to the above, there is planned recreation along with basketball, bicycle rentals with paved trails, a game room, handball, nature trails, riding stables and a 9-hole golf course beside the lake shore with rental equipment provided. There is also a lovely beach area with swimming and a nearby bathhouse.

In 1971, the Louie B. Nunn State Lodge opened in the park. Named for a former Kentucky governor, the building curves around a portion of the lake and affords an excellent view. It houses a dining room and a gift shop, meeting rooms, a lounge area and pool. Adjoining it are 51 motel-type rooms. Twelve 2-bedroom executive cottages are nearby.

On the first weekend in June, the park hosts the Glasgow Highland Games. Up to 10,000 people witness this special event celebrating Glasgow, and Kentucky's Scottish heritage.

Barren River State Resort Park is open year round.

BARREN RIVER LAKE

On a bright winter day, only at General Butler State Resort Park can one find individuals involved in snow skiing, golfing and perhaps even tennis. That is the unique quality of General Butler — there is truly something for everyone.

Located off I-75 and Kentucky 227 in Carrollton, Kentucky, General Butler State Resort Park was the first park in northern Kentucky and sixth in the state park system.

General William Orlando Butler, for whom the park is named, was a hero in the Battle of New Orleans and was on the staff of General Andrew Jackson. He married Eliza Todd, aunt of Mary Todd Lincoln, and practiced law in Carrollton where he was elected to Congress for two terms.

The Butler home on the park grounds was built in 1859. The home is a brick, federal-style eight-room residence. There is a lovely view of the Kentucky River valley from the 2-1/2 story structure,which is open for tours.

The park was first built by the Depression-era Civilian Conservation Corps. One of their finest achievements was a stone pavilion erected on the highest hill overlooking the Kentucky River. This observation point, built in irregular terraces, still stands today

Today General Butler State Resort Park consists of 791 acres. The lodge, dedicated in 1962, has grown to 57 rooms, all with private balcony or patio. There are 23 cottages ranging from efficiencies to 3-bedroom executive cabins, all furnished and with cooking facilities. There are 111 camping sites with water and electric hookups.

Recreational activities abound. There are basketball courts, boating (rowboats and paddleboats), fishing, game rooms, miniature golf, two nature trails, picnicking, play-grounds, a swimming pool, a lake with a beach, tennis, and miniature train rides. In addition to those activities, one may also tour the Butler home, or play golf on the 9-hole course. There is a Pro Shop with carts and clubs available. There is planned recreation in the summer.

General Butler is the only park in the state with a snow ski area. Begun in 1981,Ski Butler has 20 acres of ski trails, nine ski runs, and one of the most advanced snow-making machines available. On site is a ski school, chair lifts and a ski lodge containing a restaurant, shop, and rental equipment. Skiing is from December 15 to March 31.

The park is open year round. Special Events include Kentucky Scottish Weekend, where thousands gather to enjoy the Scottish traditions of music, dance and sport.

GENERAL BUTLER

Named after Kincaid Creek, Kincaid Lake was created for recreational use. It encompasses two hundred acres with five miles of shoreline. Its wooded hillsides form the setting for Kincaid Lake State Park. Located in north central Kentucky, 48 miles southeast of Covington off U.S. 27 on Kentucky 159, the 850-acre park became a part of the Kentucky Park System in 1960 when local citizens purchased the land and donated it to the state.

Kincaid Lake State Park has 84 campsites with water and electrical hookups, and primitive sites also. There is a grocery, gift shop, and multipurpose building seating 240. A recreational complex has platform tennis, basketball, shuffleboard, playgrounds, horseshoes, miniature golf, tennis, and picnic areas with shelters. There is a junior-sized olympic pool overlooking the lake with a bathhouse and sand beach. There are biking trails and three miles of nature trails. The seasonal planned recreational director oversees movies once a week at the three hundred seat amphitheater.

Kincaid Lake State Park offers a 38-slip marina. There are rental pontoons, fishing boats, rowboats and pedal boats. Fishing is for bass, bluegill, crappie and catfish.

The park is open from April 1 to October 31.

KINCAID LAKE

Kentucky's newest state park is Paintsville Lake State Park, which opened in 1986. The 242-acre park sits on the edge of Paintsville Lake. It is located in eastern Kentucky off U.S. 460 to Kentucky 40, and is four miles west of Paintsville.

The United States Army Corp of Engineers opened Paintsville Lake in May 1984. It is over twenty miles long and one hundred feet deep in places. The 1139 acre lake has clear, deep water winding through steep hills, sandstone bluffs and narrow gorges. Deer and wildlife abound. Fishermen enjoy catching largemouth, smallmouth and spotted bass, catfish, sunfish, walleye, and rainbow trout.

The full service marina, open all year, has 84 open slips, 80 covered slips, and a four lane launching ramp. For rent are houseboats, pontoons, pedal boats and fishing boats.

PAINTSVILLE LAKE

Actual burial site marker for soldiers and Indians killed at Blue Licks

The "Last Battle of the Revolution" was fought on August 19, 1782 at the present site of Blue Licks State Park. Kentucky's fifth state park was founded January 25, 1927 to commemorate that battle.

The battle, in which dozens of men of the Kentucky Militia were killed in an ambush by British soldiers and their Indian allies, was fought nearly a year after the surrender of Lord Cornwallis at Yorktown on October 19, 1781, the official ending of the Revolutionary War.

The Blue Lick Battlefield site was presented to the Kentucky State Park Commission by the Blue Lick Battlefield Monument Commission on behalf of the area citizens who had acquired and donated thirty-two acres of land. The park was formally dedicated on August 19, 1928 on the one hundred thirty-sixth anniversary of the battle of Blue Licks.

The battle monument in the park is a granite shaft on which are inscribed the names of all the dead — both Kentuckians and Indians.

The Pioneer Museum in the park today houses the collection of the T.W. Hunter, a local landowner who discovered mastadon tusks, bones and other buried artifacts in the area, as well as guns, Indian relics and other materials from the time of the battle. There are bottles, banners and labels from the springs era, a room furnished as a pioneer cabin and a seven minute audio-visual slide presentation of the Battle of Blue Licks.

The park today has grown to 148 acres. Facilities include a fifty-one site campground with water and electricity, miniature golf, pool, playgrounds, hiking trails along the Licking River, a gift shop, and a multi-purpose building for meetings. There is planned recreation in the summer

Also of interest in the park is the existence of an extremely rare plant, the Short's Goldenrod, named for Charles W. Short, a mid-19th century doctor and amateur botanist. It is the first plant in Kentucky listed as an endangered species by the United States Fish and Wildlife Service.

Special Events include a reenactment of the Battle of Blue Licks. It is held on the weekend of August 19th, the anniversary of the skirmish. The park also has a Halloween Campout, ghost-story telling, and other activities the last weekend in October.

The park is open from April 1 to October 31.

BLUE LICKS BATTLEFIELD

The world record smallmouth bass — 11 pounds, 15 ounces — was taken from the waters of Dale Hollow Lake, less than a half mile from Dale Hollow State Park.

The lake borders the Kentucky-Tennessee line twelve miles from Burkesville, Kentucky on Kentucky 449 via Kentucky 90, U.S. 127, and the Cumberland Parkway. The Flood Control Act of 1938 authorized the building of Dale Hollow Dam and Reservoir to generate electricity and control flooding. The U.S. Army Corp of Engineers built the 200 foot-high and 1717 foot-long dam in 1943. Dale Hollow Lake is 61 miles long, has 27,000 acres of water, 48 miles of surface area, 653 miles of shoreline, and measures 120 feet at its deepest point.

Located in the Cumberland foothills, the 3,398-acre Dale Hollow State Park opened in 1978. Nestled in a peninsula, the park's landscape has forests, abundant open areas and rugged hills. The second largest park in acres in the state, Kentucky leases some land from the U.S. Army Corps of Engineers, and owns the rest of the property.

The park has a marina, opened seasonally, with 36 slips and 15 buoy spaces. There is a dock and boat launching area, and pontoons and fishing boats may be rented. Fishing is good for smallmouth and white bass, crappie, rainbow trout, catfish, muskie and blugill. Also at the marina is a restaurant and a small gift shop.

Dale Hollow State Park has a 144-site campground open all year. For campers there is water, electrical hookups, grills, and three service buildings with laundry facilities. This is the only state park that allows you to bring your own horse. There are 24 sites with hitching posts and 15 miles of riding trails. A seasonal recreational director is on duty.

Also located in the park are an amphitheater, a pool, picnic areas, and playgrounds. There is an abundance of wildlife including grey and fox squirrels, wild turkey, grouse, quail, rabbit, fox, woodchuck, oppossum,raccoon and deer.

DALE HOLLOW LAKE

The most heavily stocked lake for fishing in Kentucky is Taylorsville Lake, located 45 miles southeast of Louisville off I-64, Kentucky 155 and Kentucky 44. Built by the United States Army Corp of Engineers for flood control and recreation, the lake opened in January, 1983.

Taylorsville Lake State Park opened in April, 1985. The state leased 1650 acres bordering the lake from the United States Army Corp of Engineers and named the park in honor of Richard Taylor, an early landowner and gristmill operator who donated land for the nearby town of Taylorsville.

Taylorsville Lake State Park has a full-service marina with 38 open slips and 144 covered slips. Rental pontoons, houseboats and fishing boats are available. There are several boat ramps and picnic areas. Fishing for bass, crappie, catfish, perch and bluegill is the favorite recreation. The park is open year round.

TAYLORSVILLE LAKE

Rumor has it Jesse James holed up in a cave on Rocky Creek after robbing the nearby Russellville Bank. That cave is now under Lake Malone.

The Muhlenberg County Conservation Club completed the 788-acre lake in 1960, and in 1962, 325 surrounding acres were dedicated by the state as Lake Malone State Park.

This beautiful lake has 26 miles of shoreline, magnificent sandstone cliffs such as Bear Bluff and Chalk Bluff, and a natural rock bridge. Surrounding the lake are beautiful dogwoods, mountain laurel, tall pines and hardwoods.

Lake Malone State Park has a marina with snacks, tackle, fuel, a launch ramp and a dock with forty slips. A beach and bathhouse are available for swimmers. Rental boats include fishing boats, pontoons, and rowboats. Fishing is good for rockfish, catfish, bass, bluegill, and crappie.

Also located at the park is a game court for badminton, basketball, horseshoes, shuffleboard and volleyball. There is a picnic area, shelters, a playground, a meeting room for 200, and the Mountain Laurel hiking trail. A recreational director oversees the twenty full-service campsites and one hundred primitive sites.

The campground is open from April 1 to November 15; the beach from Memorial Day to Labor Day, and the marina from April 1 until Labor Day. Lake Malone State Park is located south of Greenville, Kentucky on Kentucky 973 off U.S. 431.

LAKE MALONE

The Army Corps of Engineers began construction of an earth and random rock-filled dam on the Little Sandy River in 1964 for flood control, water quality control, recreation, and enhancement of fish and wildlife. The result was beautiful Grayson Lake.

From the dam upstream to Bruin Creek, the land is generally sloping or rolling with small cliffs. The slopes reach only 35 feet. However, up from Bruin Creek, the cliffs are more pronounced. The sheer sandstone canyons reach 50 to 150 feet in height — a truly magnificent sight. The 74.2 miles of shoreline provide excellent fishing for bass, trout, bluegill, catfish, and crappie. There is a private marina for boat rentals.

The park, situated in two counties, opened in 1970 with its 71-site campground. The Rolling Hills Campground sits above the lake and provides water and electrical hookups, two bathhouses, two playgrounds, and a walking trail by the lake. There is a seasonal recreational program, providing numerous activities in the summer, especially during the three major holidays.

Grayson Lake State Park can be reached via I-64, seven miles south of Grayson, Kentucky on Route 7. Grayson Lake State Park is open year round.

GRAYSON LAKE

In April, 1964, the Corps of Engineers began construction of a dam on the Green River for flood control. When finished in June, 1969, the dam created Green River Lake, providing 8200 acres of water recreation and 23 miles of shoreline surrounded by hills as high as 940 feet.

The campground at Green River Lake State Park is located right at the water's edge, making it one of the most popular campgrounds in the Kentucky state park system. The 156-site area has water, electrical hookups and a boat ramp. There are three bathhouses, a beach, a playground, picnic areas and shelters, a grocery store and a gift shop.

Green River Lake State Park is located in south central Kentucky, eight miles south of Campbellsville off Kentucky 55. The surrounding land is known as the Highland Rim of the Eastern Pennyroyal.

The 1331-acre Green River Lake State Park provides a beach and swimming area, a volleyball court, picnic and shelter areas, a playground, a hiking trail, and an eighteen hole miniature golf course.

A marina has a restaurant and gift shop, 110 slips, boats for rental, including pontoons, pedal boats, houseboats and fishing boats. One may fish for bass, bluegill, catfish and crappie.

The park is open all year round

GREEN RIVER LAKE

McHargue's Mill

History abounds at Levi Jackson State Park, dedicated to the struggle of pioneers during the settling of Kentucky.

John Freeman first owned the land in 1802 on which the park now stands, having received the land in payment for services during the Revolutionary War. One of the earliest settlers in Laurel County, Freeman built a large, two-story home on the Wilderness Road and in 1803 had it licensed for a tavern. His daughter, Rebecca, married Levi Jackson, Laurel County's first county judge. When Freeman died, Jackson inherited the land and renamed the tavern the Jackson Tavern. Jackson himself died July 17, 1879. His descendants donated 307 acres for the park to the state in December, 1931.

Today, reminders of history are seen throughout the park. Boone's Trace and the Wilderness Trail both run through the park. Also on the grounds is "Defeated Camp," marking the site of Kentucky's worst Indian massacre. Another historic building in the park is McHargue's Mill, on the banks of the Little Laurel River, a fully-operational mill with one of the world's largest collection of millstones.

Levi Jackson State Park also showcases the Mountain Life Museum, a reproduction of a pioneer settlement. There are seven original log structures. One is the original two room school now housing household utensils and guns. There are two cabins built in 1860, known as the Old Hopkins Home, set up to represent early pioneer life. There is a small fee to enter the museum, which is open from April to October.

Today, the recreational and historical park encompasses 896 acres on gently rolling hills. Levi Jackson State Park was the tenth park to be added to the Kentucky Park System and is open year round. The park has one of the best camping facilities in the state. There are 185 sites with water and electrical hookups. There is a community pool with snack bar and bathhouse, horseback riding, picnicking with three shelter houses, an archery range, miniature golf, and hiking on Boone's Trace and the Wilderness Road. There is a five hundred seat amphitheater with a variety of shows in the summer, and a group camp facility with fifteen cabins for two hundred people.

Special Events include the Laurel County Homecoming, a one- week annual event occuring the middle of August.

LEVI JACKSON

Kentucky River

By Daniel Boone's own account, "We proceeded on to Kentucky river . . . and on the first day of April began to erect the fort of Boonesborough at a salt lick . . . on the south side (of the river)." Over two hundred years later, people of all ages are enjoying the history and facilities at Fort Boonesborough State Park. The 153 acre park is located on Kentucky 388, just off Kentucky 627, reached by I-75. It is twelve miles north of Richmond, or ten miles southwest of Winchester.

In May, 1769 Daniel Boone began a two-year expedition to find an easier way through the mountains to locate sites for settlements. He made one attempt to settle in Kentucky in September, 1773, but was turned back by Indians. In March, 1775 he cut the Wilderness Trail and reached the Kentucky River on April 1, 1775. He began erecting a fort and in September, brought his family to live. Boone himself lived at Fort Boonesborough until 1799. During those years he was a member of the Virginia legislature and had many experiences as an explorer, frontiersman, and Indian fighter. He left with his family to go to Missouri, and eventually explored as far as Yellowstone Park. He died at the age of 82 on September 26, 1820 and is buried at Frankfort, Kentucky, overlooking the capital.

Today's fort is an accurate reconstruction of the original. Dedicated August 30, 1974, the fort is now located on higher ground, and is constructed from 10,000 southern yellow pine logs. There is a fee for entering the area, which is open from April 1 to October 31, 9 to 5:30, but closed Monday and Tuesday after Labor Day. Upon entering, there is an orientation film of the struggle to settle Kentucky's wilderness. After that, one may tour the fort, visiting each cabin. There is a museum on Daniel Boone's life and Boonesborough, a gift shop, and several cabins furnished as in Boone's day. The other cabins showcase pioneer crafts such as spinning, vegetable dying, weaving, basketry, cabinet-making, woodcarving, pottery, quilting, soap making, candle-making, folk toys, doll making, broom making and blacksmithing.

Fort Boonesborough State Park opened in 1963 with 153 acres. It is on the banks of the Kentucky River and boasts the finest sand beach in the area. There is a modern bathhouse, a sun deck, a snack bar and gift shop located in a building adjacent to the beach. Recreational facilities include a nature and historic trail, picnicking with shelter houses, riverboat cruises, a boat dock with ten slips, fishing, miniature golf, pedal boats, a playground, and basketball, volleyball, and shuffleboard courts.

The park is open year round with a 167-site campground. Water and electrical hookups are available as well as a recreational director.

Special Events include the Admiral's Day Parade. Held on Labor Day weekend, forty to fifty decorated boats cruise down the Kentucky River in front of big crowds. In October, there is the Long Rifle Championship, and a Car Show is held the second Sunday of the month.

FORT BOONESBOROUGH

The first permanent settlement west of the Alleghenies was at Fort Harrod, Kentucky. Named for James Harrod, it is located in central Kentucky in what is now the city of Harrodsburg on U.S. 68 and U.S. 127.

From 1774 to 1775 Harrod and a small group of men migrated down the Ohio, settling after several attempts in a small fort on Old Fort Hill. In September, 1775 their families came and created the first permanent settlement in Kentucky.

James Harrod at some point disappeared and his body was never found. But the fort became home and refuge to many pioneers over the years, including Daniel Boone and George Rogers Clark. The town of Harrodsburg eventually grew up around it.

In 1927, the fort was rebuilt, one third smaller and just south of the original one, and dedicated as Pioneer Memorial State Park, one of the first in the Kentucky State Park system.

Fort Harrod today recreates life in a pioneer settlement. The cabins are furnished with handmade utensils, furniture, tools and implements. Crafts persons in pioneer costume can be seen demonstrating quilting, basketry, candlemaking, broom making, woodworking, soap making, and blacksmithing.

The 22-acre park contains other interesting sights as well as the fort. There is the Mansion Museum, a Greek Revival brick home built in 1813. Inside is the Union Room, dedicated to the Union and Abraham Lincoln, and a Confederate Room dedicated to the Confederacy and its president, Jefferson Davis, a native Kentuckian. In the museum are furnishings and displays of Kentucky history, Indian relics, pioneer tools, books, documents, and musical instruments.

Also in the park are The Lincoln Marriage Temple, a brick edifice that enshrines the cabin where Abraham Lincoln's parents were married; The George Rogers Clark Memorial which Franklin D. Roosevelt dedicated in 1934 to honor all pioneers who opened up the west; The Pioneer Cemetery, the oldest cemetery west of the Alleghenies; and the James Harrod Amphitheater, for many years hosting the play "The Legend of Daniel Boone." It runs from mid-June through Labor Day every evening except Sunday.

On the grounds of Old Fort Harrod State Park are two picnic areas, a playground, shelters, a gift and craft shop, and the largest osage orange tree in the nation. Special Events include a May 1 Celebration, a Festival Weekend in June, Picnics in the Park at noon on Fridays, Oktoberfest in September, and a Halloween Ghost Tour.

The park is open all year round.

OLD FORT HARROD

Located in Louisville, E.P. "Tom" Sawyer State Park occupies 377 acres off Westport Road near the Gene Snyder Freeway. The park, in northeastern Jefferson County, was named for Erbon Powers Sawyer, a former Jefferson County Judge Executive.

The land, once owned by the Kentucky Department of Mental Health, was declared surplus in the late 1960s; in 1970 the Department of Parks obtained a lease from the state. Buildings and facilities for the park opened in 1974.

The 600-person capacity recreation building houses a gymnasium with a basketball court and areas for bad- minton, volleyball, exercise and dance classes, gymnastics, a weight room, a game area, and concessions.

The 50-meter pool is the largest in the state park system. There is a first-rate aquatics program which can accommodate over 1000 people at a time.

On the grounds can be found a one-mile cinder fitness trail with sixteen exercise stations, picnic shelters, groves, an archery range, six soccer fields, three lighted baseball diamonds and twelve all-weather tennis courts.

The park has one of the best bicycle moto-cross (BMX) tracks in the nation and has hosted the BMX Grand National Races. The park also contains a model airplane airstrip. There is a 400-foot by 35-foot paved runway for radio-controlled model planes and cars. Local and national events are held here regularly.

Special Events include a mini-triathalon and hot air balloon races.

The park is open year round with a staff to provide a multitude of recreational needs.

E.P. "TOM" SAWYER

The most heavily played golf course in the Kentucky State Park system is at Ben Hawes State Park. This recreational park features an 18-hole golf course as well as a par three 9-hole course. There is a pro shop with rental clubs and carts. It is open year round and golf tournaments are held frequently.

Besides golf, the 297-acre Ben Hawes State Park has a picnic area, three shelters, a playground, a nature trail, a softball field, archery, tennis, basketball, and a concession area.

Ben Hawes State Park is located off U.S. 60, four miles west of Kentucky's third largest city, Owensboro, an Ohio riverfront town. The park, opened in 1975, is named for a former Owensboro mayor.

BEN HAWES

The only island park in the state, General Burnside State Park is located in south central Kentucky, eight miles south of Somerset, one mile south of Burnside, Kentucky on U.S. 27. The 430 acre park, accessible by a causeway, is surrounded by Lake Cumberland, a water paradise with 1255 miles of shoreline.

The area was first called Point Isabel by Carolinians who settled here in 1800. In 1863 Ambrose Burnside, a Union Civil War general, commanded a depot here and patrolled the Cumberland River. This depot, called Camp Burnside, eventually lent its name to this state park. (Burnside also lent his name to a familiar style of men's facial hair ...that we know today as "sideburns").

Chandler Island, named for A.B. Chandler, a former

Kentucky governor, was created in the mid 1940s after Wolf Creek Dam was built on the Cumberland River, flooding the area, and creating Cumberland Lake. The Army Corp of Engineers leased the land to the state and in 1958 the park opened year round.

A six lane launching ramp is on the island and a marina is nearby for fishing and boating.

Other facilities in the park include an 18-hole golf course with pro shop, rental clubs, riding and pull carts. The hilly course is open year round. There is also a public pool with snack shop, a picnic shelter, and a playground. There is seasonal planned recreation in the 110-site campground with water and electrical hookups, showers, rest rooms and a laundry.

GENERAL BURNSIDE

The Christmas Candlelight Tour

The mansion, Federal Hill, better known as My Old Kentucky Home, was begun in 1795 and completed in 1818. Named in honor of the Federalist Party, the home has 13 windows across the front, 13 steps to each level, and 13 original rooms. It was the manor house for a large working plantation owned by Judge John Rowan, who served on the Kentucky Court of Appeals and in the U.S. Senate. Three generations of the family lived there from 1801 to 1921. Among the many guests were Henry Clay and Aaron Burr.

In 1852, Stephen Foster, a cousin of the Rowans, visited Federal Hill. Foster, a native of Pennsylvania, was a composer According to legend, while visiting Federal Hill Foster wrote "My Old Kentucky Home," which became popular during the Civil War, and later became Kentucky's state song.

In 1922 Madge Rowan Frost, the last Rowan descendant, sold Federal Hill to the state of Kentucky. A commission was organized to restore and oversee the home and grounds. On Stephen Foster's birthday, July 4, 1923, My Old Kentucky Home opened. It was not officially added to the Parks Department until 1936.

My Old Kentucky Home State Park is located in Bardstown off the Bluegrass Parkway in central Kentucky. There are tours of the home daily, with guides in period costume. There are formal gardens, a carriage house, a smokehouse, a springhouse, and a restored servant's cabin now serving as a gift shop.

The park has a forty-site campground with utilities, open April through October. A seasonal director provides recreation. There is also an 18-hole golf course with pro shop, rental carts and clubs, picnic areas with shelters, a playground, and hiking trails.

The longest-running outdoor play in the state is "The Stephen Foster Story" at My Old Kentucky Home State Park. Open since 1958, the 1400 seat amphitheater runs shows continuously from mid-June through Labor Day, Tuesday through Sunday in the evenings. This lively musical has over fifty Stephen Foster songs including "Oh Susannah," "Camptown Races," and "My Old Kentucky Home." The park also offers Candlelight Tours from Thanksgiving to Christmas.

MY OLD KENTUCKY HOME

A portrait of Stephen Foster

Stephen Foster is said to have composed "My Old Kentucky Home" on this piano and desk at Federal Hill.

Prehistoric animals roamed thousands of years ago on land now known as Big Bone Lick State Park. Located in north central Kentucky near Walton on Kentucky 338, it is twenty miles southwest of the Covington-Newport area.

Giant mastodons, mammoths, bison, primitive horses, sloths, and giant stag-moose came to the "jelly-ground," as the soft area was called by the pioneers, to quench their thirst and satisfy their need for salt and minerals. Often the animals became mired in the soft ground and died. Over thousands of years the bones turned to stone.

Big Bone Lick was the first widely-known collecting locality for Ice Age bones in North America. In 1739, the bones were first discovered by Charles Le Moyne, second Baron DeLongueil, a French Canadian explorer and soldier. He was followed by Robert Smith, an Indian trader, who in 1744 removed the first fossils, and in 1752 by John Findley, a Kentucky settler who visited the Shawnee Indians.

Lewis and Clark collected over 300 bones on their voyage west, sending them to President Thomas Jefferson at the White House.

The area also was important to Indians and pioneers because of the warm sulphur springs and salt — a necessity for food preservation. In 1780 a crude fort was built for protection of salt expeditions. In the 1800s health spas sprang up. Wealthy southern families came to socialize and take the "curative qualities" of the springs.

On August 25, 1953 a Historical Society adopted resolutions urging the establishment of a state park at Big Bone. In December, 1960, the Department of Parks announced plans to construct roads and build picnic areas and shelters on the land.

Today the park encompasses 525 acres. Where once was swampland, now are wildflowers and brush. There are forty acres of picnic grounds, and a 62-site campground with electricity, grill, water, showers, rest rooms, laundry, and a pool. There is a grocery store and gift shop. Planned recreation occurs in the summer with basketball, volleyball and tennis courts, a softball field, a horseshoe pit, hiking trails, a playground and miniature golf. The seven-acre lake has fishing for catfish, bass and bluegill.

The indoor-outdoor museum in the park has displays of ancient bones and a video show about the history of Big Bone Lick. Outside are lifesize models of prehistoric mastadons and bison, and a model "dig" display.

Special Events at Big Bone Lick State Park include the Salt Festival in October, where salt-making is demonstrated In the spring the Flying Cardinals sponsor a show of remote controlled flying objects.

BIG BONE LICK

On the bluffs of the Mississippi River, in the Jackson Purchase area of Kentucky, sits Columbus-Belmont State Park. The area was discovered by the French explorers Marquette and Joliet in 1673, and named "Iron Banks" for the iron deposits found on the bluffs.

Because of its strategic location, the bluffs became a focal point during the Civil War. The Confederates, led by General Leonidas Polk, seized the area on September 3, 1861 and heavily fortified the bluffs. Earthen trenches were built, and 140 heavy guns and cannons were placed along the river. A mile-long chain, each link weighing twenty pounds and held by a six ton anchor, was laid across the Mississippi River on pontoons to the Missouri side, called Camp Belmont. This prevented Union gunboats from controlling the Missisippi River. Confederate soldiers, numbering 19,000, turned the area into Fort DeRussey. It was the most fortified area in North America and was called the "Gibralter of the West."

The Union, realizing the value of the bluffs, set about taking it. General Grant, in his first major battle, brought his troops in behind Camp Belmont, attacked, and declared victory on November 7, 1861. However, in celebrating their first victory, the Union allowed the Confederate prisoners to escape. They regrouped and formed with soldiers from Fort DeRussey to retake Camp Belmont.

In March, 1862, the Union finally re-occupied Fort DeRussey. The area remained a garrison and supply base for the Federals until 1870.

In 1927, a great flood occurred. The town of Columbus was flooded, forcing it to move one mile to higher ground. The water dug into the bluffs, exposing the all-but-forgotten river chain. The people of the area decided to preserve this bit of history and bought the acres of former Fort DeRussey. In 1934, the state purchased the land and formed Columbus-Belmont State Park.

Today, the 156-acre park has on display the anchor and part of the mighty chain. Housed in an 1850 home that was used as an infirmary by the Confederates, is a museum. There is an audio-visual presentation of the battle, Civil War relics, Indian artifacts, and displays of the history of the area. Easily recognizable are the trenches and earthworks the army used. Also on the park grounds are picnic areas, a playground, miniature golf, a concession stand, a gift shop and two and one-half miles of hiking trails. A campground has 38 sites with water and electricity. The views of the Mississippi River are spectacular.

Columbus-Belmont State Park is located 36 miles southwest of Paducah on Kentucky 123. It is open every day from April 1 to October 31.

COLUMBUS-BELMONT

John James Audubon, the celebrated artist/ornithologist, came to America at the age of eighteen. His study of birds and other wild creatures largely took place in Kentucky.

The Henderson, Kentucky Audubon Society was formed in 1898 to preserve his memory. Through the efforts of local citizens, land was bought, deeded to the state and on October 3, 1938, John James Audubon State Park was begun. The Civil Conservation Corps constructed the park. They built the gate, house, gardens, shelter houses, trails, cabins, wildlife area, picnic areas, lake and museum. Today the buildings and grounds are on the National Historic Register.

The Audubon Memorial Museum is the focal point of the Park. It is built of native stone and designed as a reproduction of a French Norman Inn, in honor of Audubon's French heritage. There is a French garden and cobbled courtyard. Inside are priceless original prints from the double-elephant (27" x 40") folio collection of "The Birds of America" published in 1926, many of Audubon's original oils and watercolors, personal items, furniture, and memorabilia.

The park is located in Henderson off U.S. 41 on the northwest edge of Kentucky. The 619 acres feature rolling wooded hills, sheltered valleys, and an abundance of plant life, making it a natural bird sanctuary.

The park contains 5.7 miles of hiking trails and the nine mile Audubon Trail. On the 28-acre lake there is a beach, swim area, bathhouse, and boat dock. One may rent pedal boats and also fish for bass, bluegill, and catfish.

Other recreational facilities include picnic areas with shelters, a playground, tennis courts, a nature center, a gift shop, and a nine-hole golf course with pro shop and rental clubs and carts. A seasonal recreational director is available from April 1 to October 31.

Open year round are five one-bedroom cottages, and the 64-site campground with water and electrical hookups.

JOHN JAMES AUDUBON

Abraham Lincoln's family heritage is commemorated in Lincoln Homestead State Park. The park is located in central Kentucky, five miles north of Springfield off U.S. 150 on Kentucky 528.

Captain Abraham Lincoln, grandfather of the President, obtained one hundred acres of land in Kentucky and settled in this area in 1782.

After Captain Lincoln's death at the hands of Indians while clearing land, Thomas Lincoln, his son and the President's father, lived here off and on until the age of 25. He was raised in a cabin at this location on a creek that became known as Lincoln's Run.

After a succession of private owners, the land was donated to the state, and a park was created in 1936.

The living museum on the grounds contains several buildings. The first is a replica of the Lincoln cabin, recreated on the exact spot where Thomas Lincoln was raised. The 1782 cabin near the Beech Fork River has logs over one hundred years old. Some of the pioneer pieces inside the cabin were made by Thomas Lincoln himself. A split rail fence surrounds the area.

Also on the premises is the actual building where Nancy Hanks, the mother of Abraham Lincoln, lived when Thomas Lincoln proposed to her. The cabin, moved one mile from its original location to become part of the park, belonged to the Berry family. Inside the cabin is a copy of the marriage bond between Lincoln and Hanks.

A reproduction of the Berry blacksmith shop is situated behind the Lincoln cabin. A fieldstone enclosure on the grounds, placed by the Federal government, is a memorial to Nancy Hanks.

The 140-acre park has a gift shop, picnic shelters, play areas and an 18-hole golf course with pro shop, rental clubs and carts, and snack bar. Tournaments are held all year.

LINCOLN HOMESTEAD

The park with the highest elevation in the state of Kentucky is Kingdom Come State Park, established in 1962. It is located at the top of Pine Mountain on the border of Virginia and Kentucky, 50 miles northeast of Middlesboro via U.S. 25E and U.S. 119 to Cumberland. The mountain views are spectacular, the scenery gorgeous, and the geological rock formations are unusual and interesting.

Pine Mountain's 1200 acres are located at or above 2500 feet in elevation. The park got its name from the novel "The Little Shepherd of Kingdom Come," the first book in the United States to sell one million copies. It was written by John Fox, a native Kentuckian who lived his adult life in this area.

The park is set midway on the Little Shepherd Trail, which winds 38 miles from Harlan to Whitesburg. Originally started in the 1930s as a fire road, the trail is a narrow gravel path accessible by car or foot.

Kingdom Come State Park has seven overlooks. "Bullock," "Creech" and "12 o'clock" face the north and are the most popular. There are also beautiful rock formations in the park, the most famous of which, Raven's Rock, is a gigantic sandstone slab 290 feet high.

A gazebo at the park overlooks the south where Big Black Mountain, the tallest peak in the state at over 4000 feet, can be seen.

In the park there is a three-acre lake where pedal boats are available for fishing for bass, bluegill, crappie and trout. Also available are seven miles of hiking trails, three playgrounds, picnicing with two shelters, and miniature golf.

KINGDOM COME

The greatest Civil War battle in Kentucky was fought on October 8, 1862 in the area now called the Perryville Battlefield State Shrine.

Union General Don Carlos Buell's troops faced the armies of Confederate Generals Kirby-Smith and Bragg outside the town of Perryville. After a furious battle, the Confederates, after an early advantage, retreated, leaving the state of Kentucky to the Federals.

After the battle, the Union buried its dead in a field. The bodies later were moved to Camp Nelson National Cemetery. The locals buried the Confederates in four common graves and added a square stone wall around it.

Originally called Perryville National Cemetery, the 98-acre area became a state park in 1928. Inside the wall, in the center of the cemetery, a monument was built in 1902 to honor the Confederate soldiers. In 1931, the Federal government built a monument several yards away to honor the Union soldiers. There are also various state monuments on the grounds.

A museum in the park has an audio-visual presentation of the battle, as well as a map, a diorama, war relics and displays. A small fee is charged. A walking self tour and a driving tour are offered to help understand the battle.

Perryville Battlefield State Shrine holds a battle reenactment the closest weekend to October 8 each year. The actual battle is recreated, with camps, drills and demonstrationson display. Several hundred men participate, and several thousand attend this living history event.

The park also has a gift shop, picnic areas and a playground. It is open daily from April 1 to October 31 and is located off U.S. 60 and U.S. 150, two miles north of Perryville.

PERRYVILLE BATTLEFIELD

Jefferson Davis, president of the Confederacy from 1861 to 1865, was born on June 3, 1808 in what is now Fairview, Kentucky. His father was given land there for military service. The land proved to be rocky, and when Jefferson Davis was a year old the family moved to Mississippi seeking better land.

Because of his birthplace in Kentucky, ironically less than 100 miles from the birthplace of his Civil War adversary, Abraham Lincoln, the United Daughters of the Confederacy raised funds through private donations to honor Jefferson Davis. A stone fence was placed around seventeen chosen acres and a monument in the shape of an obelisk was begun in 1917. In 1924 the monument was dedicated and turned over to the state as a park.

The obelisk was a wonder of its time, and is still visible for miles. It is 351 feet tall with a 35-foot by 35-foot base. The concrete walls are ten feet thick at the bottom tapering to two feet at the top. It is the tallest concrete obelisk in the world and the fourth tallest monument in the United States. Inside is an elevator, originally run by steam, taking visitors to the top for a spectacular view of the countryside.

The park, open from May 1 to October 31, is located ten miles east of Hopkinsville on U.S. 68. In addition to the monument there is a gift shop, playground and picnic areas. On the first Sunday of June each year the park celebrates Jefferson Davis's birthday with a Civil War re-enactment.

JEFFERSON DAVIS MONUMENT

The "Lion of White Hall" is a term used to describe Cassius Marcellus Clay, a Kentucky abolitionist Congressman and statesman. Whitehall, his home, is now a state historic shrine. The Italianate mansion has over thirty rooms, covers 9,000 square feet, and has 16 foot ceilings and seven levels.

Clay died in 1903 and left his properties to the federal government. Since he had not paid taxes for several years, the government ordered an auction to pay his debts. Two of his grandchildren bought the house and land and rented it to tenants until 1966. The home was vandalized and in a sad state of repair, when in July, 1968 the state bought the house and pledged to restore it. After the state purchased the house original furnishings were discovered, including two portraits — one of Russian Czar Alexander II and one of a Russian ballerina, both accumulated while Clay was Ambassador to Russia. An 1859 Steinway grand piano, once used in the ballroom, was returned. In September, 1971 White Hall was opened to the public.

Today the park is open from April 1 to October 31. There is a gift shop and a picnic area. Also on the grounds are several original outbuildings, including a blacksmith shop, gristmill, corncrib, smokehouse, chicken house, ice house, kitchen and former slave quarters. At a distance, one can see a picket fence protecting the old family cemetery.

The park is located two miles off I-75 at exit 95 near Richmond, Kentucky in the central region of Kentucky.

WHITE HALL

The smallest park in the Kentucky state park system is the Isaac Shelby State Historic Site. In 1951, the one-half acre burial ground of the Shelby family was given to the state as a shrine. The 1820 secluded cemetery, surrounded by a stone wall, contains the burial site and monument of Kentucky's first governor,Isaac Shelby, and the 22 graves of his wife and family. Located off U.S. 127, five miles south of Danville, the site is open year round from 10 to 3 during the week.

ISAAC SHELBY CEMETERY

In 1750 Dr. Thomas Walker was employed by the Loyal Land Grant Company in Virginia to explore 800,000 acres in "Kentucke." After locating a gap in the mountains, which he named Cumberland Gap for the Duke of Cumberland, he arrived near the banks of the Cumberland River, also named by him for the Duke on April 23, 1750.

Dr. Walker stayed in this location for about a week, laying claim to the land by building a small cabin, before returning to Virginia on July 13, 1750. He never returned, and it was not until 1769 that a more famous explorer, Daniel Boone, came through the Gap and settled Kentucky.

Today, a replica of that first cabin in Kentucky, supposedly on the original site, comprises the Dr. Thomas Walker State Historic Site. Located six miles southwest of Barbourville on Ky. 459 off U.S. 25E, the Site encompasses 12 acres.

In addition to the log cabin, there is miniature golf, a picnic area, a basketball court, a playground, a gift and snack shop, and a monument to Walker's memory.

The grounds are open year round, but the facilities are open only from March 15 to October 15.

DR. THOMAS WALKER

The oldest log meeting house in Kentucky is called the Old Mulkey Meeting House. It is found three miles south of Tompkinsville on Kentucky 1446, 50 miles southeast of Bowling Green in south central Kentucky. The Old Mulkey Meeting House became a state park in 1931.

Settlers came from the Carolinas in 1773 to this area of Kentucky, led by Philip Mulkey. A focal point of the park today, the meeting house built in 1804 by Philip Mulkey's grandson, John, is fifty feet long, thirty feet wide, with wood shingles, five windows and three doors. There are twelve corners to the building, said to represent the Twelve Disciples; the three doors represent the Trinity. The building is shaped in the form of a cross.

On the grounds of the meeting house is a graveyard. Daniel Boone's sister, Hannah is buried here, as are fifteen Revolutionary War soldiers.

The sixty-acre park is open year round. There are picnic facilities with shelters, a grill and a playground.

OLD MULKEY MEETINGHOUSE

On June 1, 1792 a constitution was adopted and signed, making Kentucky the fifteenth state to enter the Union. This momentous event took place at a site now known as the Constitution Square Historic Site. Located in the heart of Danville, via U.S. 127 and U.S. 150, this three-acre park was established in 1937 and dedicated in 1942.

Today there is a self-guided tour to view the structures and learn the history of Kentucky's first courthouse square.

Three reconstructed buildings are in the park. The log courthouse was first built in 1785. The jail, built around 1785, has nine-inch thick logs. The original post office still stands. Built before 1792, this log cabin was the first post office west of the Alleghenies. Fisher's Row contains two two-story brick houses joined by a wall. They were built in 1817 as rental property. Adjacent is the Watts-Bell House, built in 1816-1817 by William Watts for Joshua Bell, a local merchant.

The 1820s schoolhouse, originally two rooms constructed of brick, is now renovated as a home. Grayson's Tavern, a two story building constructed in 1785 is where many of the constitutional convention meetings took place. Behind it is the summer kitchen.

Governor's Circle sits in the middle of the park and is a memorial to Kentucky's first governor, Isaac Shelby. Another monument in the park is dedicated to the family who gave this land to the state.

Housed in some of the buildings are a gift shop, an art league and a historical society. Special Events include the Constitution Square Festival the third week in September, with food, arts and crafts and entertainment. The first week in December is a Christmas Festival with music, and arts and crafts.

CONSTITUTION SQUARE

The oldest brick house west of the Alleghenies is the William Whitley House, located south of Lexington on Route 150, just east of Highway 127 near Stanford. It became a State Historic Shrine in 1951.

A son of Irish immigrants, William Whitley was an explorer from Virginia who made his first trip to Kentucky in 1775 with his brother-in-law, George Rogers Clark. Over the years that followed he accumulated 2800 acres of land as a reward for Indian fighting, and began building a brick home around 1787.

Travelers moving west would stop, it is told, to do work on the house, and would be rewarded by Whitley with acres of land. The bricks were fired on the premises, and varied in color due to the varying degrees of heat in the firing kiln. Light colored bricks can be seen today in the initials W.W. on the front of the house, E.W. (for wife Esther Whitley) on the back.

Indian attacks were always a possibility, so many features of the house were designed for security. Rifles and gunpowder stores were kept in cabinets by the fireplace. There are few windows, with one room being windowless so the women and children would be safe. There is a secret staircase leading to the second floor.

The house came to be known as the "Guardian of Wilderness Road," and was a welcome respite for weary travelers, whose numbers include Isaac Shelby, Kentucky's first Governor, Daniel Boone and George Rogers Clark.

After an oval race track was built in 1788, the first in Kentucky, the home became known as "Sportsman's Hill."

Today the Whitley House State Shrine honors his memory. The park contains a playground, picnic areas, and a gift shop in the old kitchen cabin. The park is open all year from 9 until 5, with the exception of Monday's between September and May. There is a small fee to tour the house.

WILLIAM WHITLEY HOUSE

Waves of bluegrass blowing in the wind inspired Joseph Bryan Sr. (1797-1887) to name his 2000 acre plantation "Waveland", built in 1847. The large L-shaped Greek Revival antebellum mansion with its gigantic Ionic columns, high-ceiling rooms, spacious hallways and verandas is very significant architecturally and historically to the state of Kentucky.

Located five miles south of Lexington on Higbee Mill Road, the property was first surveyed by Daniel Boone for his nephew, Daniel Boone Bryan (1758-1845).

In time the house was sold to a series of private individuals until 1956, when the Commonwealth of Kentucky bought the land to use as an experimental farm for the University of Kentucky. In 1957, Waveland was designated a Kentucky Life Museum, and in 1971 it was deeded to the Kentucky Department of Parks.

Today the park is situated on 10 acres. The home and grounds are open for tours, which last approximately 45 minutes. The concept of Waveland is to depict Kentucky life in the 1840s, concentrating on social customs, agriculture, decorative arts, and family stories. Inside the house are displays of china, silver, toys, clothing, tools, utensils, and military relics. Outside there is a flower garden, featuring older varieties of flowers, an herb garden, and a nature trail.

Outbuildings include brick servants' quarters, a country store, a craft shop, a smokehouse and an ice house.

Special Events include a Civil War re-enactment and a Christmas Candlelight Tour.

Waveland is open from March 1 to December 31, Tuesday through Saturday 10 a.m. to 4 p.m.. Waveland is at 225 Higbee Mill Road, Lexington, Kentucky 40503.

WAVELAND

The only theme park in the world exclusively dedicated to the horse is the Kentucky Horse Park, located in the beautiful bluegras region of central Kentucky. It is in the area known as the horse capital of the world, outside of Lexington, Kentucky on Iron Works Pike.

The Kentucky Horse Park is managed by the Tourism Cabinet of the Commonwealth of Kentucky, but as a separate agency, run by a governing body appointed by the governor.

The Kentucky Horse Park exists on land originally granted by Patrick Henry, Governor of Virginia, to his brother-in-law, William Christian, in 1777, as a reward for military service. The land has changed ownership many times over the years, but the best-known of the farms was called Walnut Hall and was one of the largest and best known Standardbred farms in America. On December 15, 1972, the 1032 acre farm was sold to the Commonwealth of Kentucky.

The Kentucky Horse Park now comprises 62 buildings, show rings, barns, stalls, a race track, an indoor stadium, and many other facilities for most events related to the horse. Visitors can eaily spend a day enjoying all types of equine entertainment.

Also on the grounds is the International Museum of the Horse. The 52,000 square feet of space is dedicated to all breeds of horse and to man's continued relationship to horses. The museum covers fifty million years of equine history.

In addition to the self-guided Walking Farm Tour there are pony rides, trail rides, horse-drawn tours and surrey rides. At the Hall of Champions, some of the greatest competitive horses to ever race are shown daily. There are bronze statues of Man o' War and Secretariat, two of the greatest horses of all time. A gift shop and restaurant is also available.

The United States Polo Association is headquartered at the Kentucky Horse Park. There are six polo fields and matches are held every Sunday,from June to October. The Kentucky Equine Institute is housed at the park. Students learn care, training, and handling of horses. The American Saddle Horse Museum is also on the park grounds.

Many Special Events are held at the Kentucky Horse Park. There are shows there almost every weekend throughout the spring, summer, and fall.

The campgrounds are open year round. There are 260 sites with water and electricity. The grounds have a grocery, gift shop, pool, lighted courts for basketball and volleyball, horseshoes, croquet, tennis, playground, and planned recreation.

KENTUCKY HORSE PARK

Shaker Village of Pleasant Hill is run by a non-profit, educational corporation to preserve and maintain the site of the Shaker community at Pleasant Hill, Kentucky. Thirty original buildings feature Shaker crafts, craftspeople and other interpretations of the life of the Shakers. There is overnight lodging, fine dining, and a gift shop. The Shaker Village is located seven miles northeast of Harrodsburg off U.S. 68.

SHAKER VILLAGE OF PLEASANT HILL

Cumberland Gap National Historic Park features a panoramic view of the gap through the mountains which paved the way for travel to the west.

There is a visitor's center. It is located south of Middlesboro on U.S. 25E.

CUMBERLAND GAP

At Breaks Interstate Park there are 4500 acres for exploring the deepest gorge east of the Mississippi, hiking trails, a restaurant, lodging, and camping. Created jointly by the states of Kentucky and Virginia, it is located on the boundary of these two states.

THE BREAKS

At the Abraham Lincoln Birthplace National Historic Site a granite memorial shrine encases a log cabin, traditionally believed to be the birthplace of Abraham Lincoln. It is located three miles south of Hodgensville off U.S. 31E.

ABRAHAM LINCOLN'S BIRTHPLACE

Mammoth Cave National Park features the longest known cave system in the world, with over 300 miles of explored passageways. Activities include a Visitor's Center, several tours of the caves, overnight lodging, camping, hiking and dining. It is located off I-65 from Cave City or Park City.

MAMMOTH CAVE

At Big South Fork National River and Recreational Area there are approximately 100,000 acres of natural wilderness to enjoy. Activities include exploring the Blue Heron Mining Community (a company-built mining camp of the 1930s, complete with mine), the Scenic Railway, campgrounds, whitewater rafting, canoeing, hiking, hunting, and fishing. It is located in southeastern Kentucky.

BIG SOUTH FORK

Land Between the Lakes was developed by TVA on 170,000 wooded acres between Lake Barkley and Kentucky Lake in western Kentucky. Activities include a Visitor Center, The Homeplace 1850 (a living history farm), a woodlands nature center (wildlife exhibits), hiking trails, hunting, camping, and fishing.

LAND BETWEEN THE LAKES

PARK ADDRESSES

Abraham Lincoln Birthplace
National Historic Site
US-31E
Hodgenville, Kentucky 42748

Barren River Lake State Resort Park
Route 1, Box 191
Lucas, Kentucky 42156-9709

Ben Hawes State Park
Box 761
Owensboro, Kentucky 42302-0761

Big Bone Lick State Park
3380 Beaver Road
Union, Kentucky 41091-9627

Big South Fork
P.O. Drawer 630
Oneida, Tennesse 37841

Blue Licks Battlefield State Park
P.O. Box 66
Mount Olivet, Kentucky 41064-0066

Breaks Interstate Park
P.O. Box 100
Breaks, Virginia 24607

Buckhorn Lake State Resort Park
HC 36, Box 1000
Buckhorn, Kentucky 41721-9602

Carter Caves State Resort Park
Route 5, Box 1120
Olive Hill, Kentucky 41164-9032

Columbus Belmont Battlefield State Park
P.O. Box 8
Columbus, Kentucky 42032-0008

Constitution Square State Historic Site
105 E. Walnut Street
Danville, Kentucky 40422-1817

Cumberland Falls State Resort Park
Route 6, Box 411
Corbin, Kentucky 40701-8814

Cumberland Gap National Historical Park
Box 1848
Middlesboro, Kentucky 40965-1848

Dale Hollow Lake State Park
6371 State Park Road
Bow, Kentucky 42714-9728

Dr. Thomas Walker State Historic Site
HC 83, Box 868
Barbourville, Kentucky 40906-9603

E.P. "Tom" Sawyer State Park
3000 Freys Hill Road
Louisville, Kentucky 40241-2172

Fort Boonesborough State Park
4375 Boonesborough Road
Richmond, Kentucky 40475-9316

General Burnside State Park
P.O. Box 488
Burnside, Kentucky 42519-0488

General Butler State Resort Park
Box 325
Carrollton, Kentucky 41008-0325

Grayson Lake State apark
Route 3, Box 415
Olive Hill, Kentucky 41164-9213

Greenbo Lake State Resort Park
HC 60, Box 562
Greenup, Kentucky 41144-9517

Green River Lake State Park
179 Park Office Road
Campbellsville, Kentucky 42718-9351

Isaac Shelby Cemetery State Historic Site
Danville, Kentucky 40422

Jefferson Davis Monument State Historic Site
P.O. Box 10
Fairview, Kentucky 42221-0010

Jenny Wiley State Resort Park
HC 66, Box 200
Prestonburg, Kentucky 41653-9799

John James Audubon State Park
P.O. Box 576
Henderson, Kentucky 42420-0576

Kenlake State Resort Park
Route 1, Box 522
Hardin, Kentucky 42048-9737

Kentucky Dam Village State Resort Park
P.O. Box 69
Gilbertsville, Kentucky 42044-0069

Kentucky Horse Park
4089 Iron Works Pike
Lexington, Kentucky 40511

Kincaid Lake State Resort
Route 4, Box 33
Falmouth, Kentucky 41040-9203

Kingdom Come State Park
Box M
Cumberland, Kentucky 40823-0420

Lake Barkley State Resort Park
Box 790
Cadiz, Kentucky 42211-0790

Lake Cumberland State Resort Park
P.O. Box 380
Jamestown, Kentucky 42629-0380

Lake Malone State Park
Dunmor, Kentucky 42339

Land Between The Lakes

100 Van Morgan Drive
Golden Pond, Kentucky 42211-9001

Levi Jackson State Park
998 Levi Jackson Mill Road
London, Kentucky 40741-8944

Lincoln Homestead State Park
Route 1 Box 3413
Springfield, Kentucky 40069-9606

Mammoth Cave National Park
Mammoth Cave, Kentucky 42259

My Old Kentucky Home State Park
P.O. Box 323
Bardstown, Kentucky 40004-0323

Natural Bridge State Resort Park
General Delivery
Slade, Kentucky 40376-9999

Old Fort Harrod State Park
P.O. Box 156
Harrodsburg, Kentucky 40330-0156

Old Mulkey Meetinghouse State Historic Site
Route 1, Box 539
Tompkinsville, Kentucky 42167-8766

Paintsville Lake State Park
General Delivery
Staffordsville, Kentucky 41256

Pennyrile Forest State Resort Park
20781 Pennyrile Lodge Road
Dawson Springs, Kentucky 42408-9212

Perryville Battlefield State Historic Site
General Delivery
Perryville, Kentucky 40468

Pine Mountain State Resort Park
1050 State Park Road
Pineville, Kentucky 40977-0610

Rough River State Resort Park
Route 1, Box 1
Falls of Rough, Kentucky 40119-9701

Shaker Village of Pleasant Hill
3500 Lexington Road
Harrodsburg, Kentucky 40330

Taylorsville Lake State Park
P.O. Box 509
Taylorsville, Kentucky 40071-0509

Waveland State Historic Site
225 Higbee Mill Road
Lexington, Kentucky 40503-4778

White Hall State Historic Site
500 White Hall Shrine Road
Richmond, Kentucky 40475-9159

William Whitley House State Historic Site
Route 1, Box 232
Stanford, Kentucky 40484-9752

RESORT PARKS - These parks contain everything a visitor needs for an extended vacation. There is overnight lodging in the form of rooms and cottages, campgrounds, dining, and a wide variety of recreational activities. Most contain a golf course and are situated on a lake for boating, fishing and swimming. Their natural settings in the mountains or on one of Kentucky's beautiful lakes provide beautiful, restful surroundings.

RECREATIONAL PARKS - These are similar in nature to the Resort Parks, except that they provide only campgrounds, with no overnight lodging or dining facilities. Most of these parks are situated on a lake for convenient water activities.

STATE HISTORIC SITES - These parks are small in acreage, but hold some historical significance.

NATIONAL PARKS - Kentucky has a wide variety of National Parks, National Historical Sites, National Recreational areas, and National Forests.

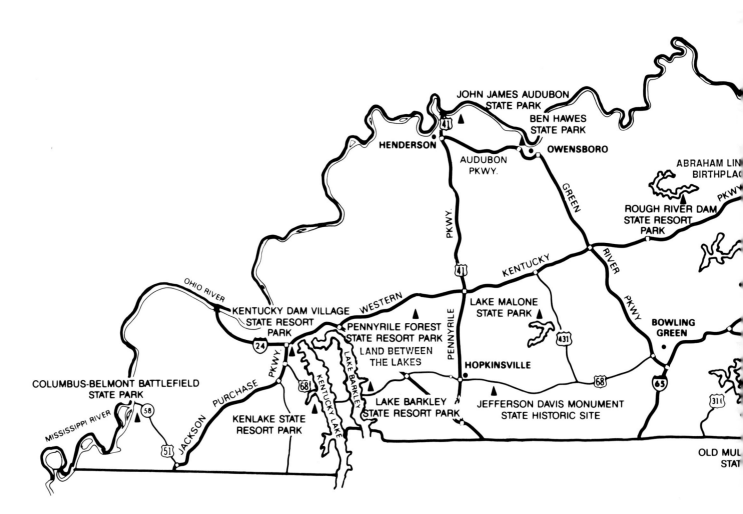

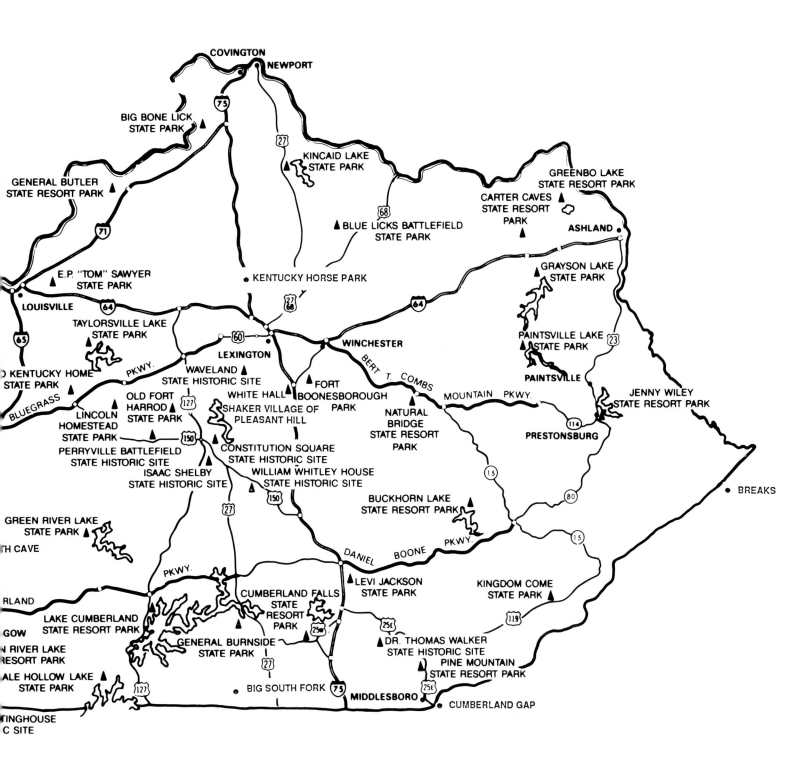

COVINGTON
NEWPORT
75

BIG BONE LICK
STATE PARK

27
KINCAID LAKE
STATE PARK

GREENBO LAKE
STATE RESORT PARK

GENERAL BUTLER
STATE RESORT PARK

CARTER CAVES
STATE RESORT
PARK

68
BLUE LICKS BATTLEFIELD
STATE PARK

ASHLAND

71

E.P. "TOM" SAWYER
STATE PARK

KENTUCKY HORSE PARK

GRAYSON LAKE
STATE PARK

64

LOUISVILLE
64

TAYLORSVILLE LAKE
STATE PARK

27
68

WINCHESTER

PAINTSVILLE LAKE
STATE PARK
23

65

D KENTUCKY HOME
STATE PARK

60
LEXINGTON

WAVELAND
STATE HISTORIC SITE

BERT T. COMBS

PAINTSVILLE

PKWY.

WHITE HALL

FORT
BOONESBOROUGH
PARK

MOUNTAIN PKWY.

JENNY WILEY
STATE RESORT PARK

BLUEGRASS

OLD FORT
HARROD
STATE PARK

127

SHAKER VILLAGE OF
PLEASANT HILL

NATURAL
BRIDGE
STATE RESORT
PARK

114

PRESTONSBURG

LINCOLN
HOMESTEAD
STATE PARK

150

CONSTITUTION SQUARE
STATE HISTORIC SITE

PERRYVILLE BATTLEFIELD
STATE HISTORIC SITE

ISAAC SHELBY
STATE HISTORIC SITE

WILLIAM WHITLEY HOUSE
STATE HISTORIC SITE

15

150

BREAKS

GREEN RIVER LAKE
STATE PARK

27

BUCKHORN LAKE
STATE RESORT PARK

80

15

TH CAVE

PKWY.

DANIEL   BOONE   PKWY.

RLAND

LEVI JACKSON
STATE PARK

KINGDOM COME
STATE PARK

GOW

LAKE CUMBERLAND
STATE RESORT PARK

CUMBERLAND FALLS
STATE
RESORT
PARK

25W

25E

119

N RIVER LAKE
RESORT PARK

GENERAL BURNSIDE
STATE PARK

27

DR. THOMAS WALKER
STATE HISTORIC SITE

ALE HOLLOW LAKE
STATE PARK

127

BIG SOUTH FORK

75

MIDDLESBORO

PINE MOUNTAIN
STATE RESORT PARK

25E

TINGHOUSE
C SITE

CUMBERLAND GAP

PHOTOGRAPHIC CREDITS

SAM ABELL 6-7, 84, 86, 103,

JAMES ARCHAMBAULT 12, 16, 22, 38, 39, 60 (bottom), 64 (top), 106,

GARY S. CHAPMAN 32, 33

BILL FORTNEY 25 (top), 37 (bottom),

ADAM JONES 23, 24, 25 (bottom)

KENTUCKY DEPARTMENT OF PARKS 20, 29, 42 (Jean E. Unglaub), 45, 47, 59, 63 (bottom), 68, 71, 72, 73, 80, 88 (Jean E. Unglaub), 102 (Jean E. Unglaub)

KENTUCKY DEPARTMENT OF TRAVEL DEVELOPMENT   Cover, 2-3, 4-5, 10-11, 21, 26-27, 28 (Dan Dry), 30, 31, 34, 40, 41, 43 (2), 49, 50-51 (Dan Dry), 58, 60 (top), 62, 70 (bottom), 79, 87 (Dan Dry), 89, 99, 107

KENNETH HAYDEN 74-75, 76, 77 (left), 82, 83, 94, 95

JIM ROBINSON 70 (top)

SCOTT T. SMITH 54

PAM SPAULDING 35, 36, 37 (top)

WILLIAM STRODE 8-9, 15, 18, 44, 46, 48, 52, 53, 55, 56-57 (3), 61, 63 (top), 64 (bottom), 65, 66, 67, 69, 77 (right), 78, 81, 85, 90 (2), 91, 92, 93, 96, 97, 98, 100, 101, 104, 105 (2), 108